Royston
in old picture postcards volume 2

by F. John Smith B. Sc.
Member of North Hertfordshire District Council
and of Royston & District Local History Society

European Library   ZALTBOMMEL / THE NETHERLANDS

I dedicate this volume to my wife Ann, who has always been so
supportive of my interests in Royston.

GB ISBN 90 288 6267 6

© 1996 European Library – Zaltbommel/The Netherlands

Introduction

My first volume of photographs of Royston in this series was published in 1983 and was received with much interest, both by present residents of the town and by former inhabitants who wanted to refresh their memories of where they had once lived. Copies went as far afield as America and Australia. This second volume has been planned along similar lines without, I hope, repeating myself.

None of these pictures is earlier than about 1890. Since that time a sleepy market town has been transformed into a thriving community based upon light industry and people commuting to work elsewhere, including many travelling each day by train to London. The population has therefore grown from around 3,500 in 1896 to about 15,000 in 1996. The town has nevertheless remained recognisably the same place, because the pattern of the core has stayed unaltered.

The biggest change over the last one hundred years is, however, the effect of the motor car. No street is a quiet backwater today, whereas at the end of the 19th century very little traffic was to be seen even in the main thoroughfares. Many buildings of interest were demolished in the centre to pander to the growth of road transport; we are fortunate that many more were saved and that conservation and listing of notable buildings is now the accepted practice.

All the same, Royston is a better place to live in today than it was a century ago, at least in purely physical terms. There is decent housing for all, whereas much of the accommodation in late Victorian times consisted of hovels, considered by our current standards. We have a modern sewage works to replace the primitive facilities that used to exist. The town is skirted by a by-pass to remove much through traffic and the railway has been electrified (although the service to London is not much quicker than it was a century ago). The schools are excellent and leisure facilities have multiplied – take, for example, the cinema, the swimming pool, the Coombes Community Centre, the Royston & District Museum, the Heath Sports Club, etc.

People remain much the same. Roystonians old and new retain a sense of pride in their unique community, and societies interested in cultural activities are strong. The Royston & District Local History Society has now been active for more than a quarter of a century. Each winter it holds a well-attended series of lectures. More importantly perhaps, it has been the spur to the formation of the Royston & District Museum, which operates under the aegis of the Royston Town Council. What is more, the Society provides guides to the Royston Cave and the Friends of the Museum is its daughter organisation.

I remain confident that the town will continue to deserve its Latin motto: *A bonis ad meliora*, which being translated becomes: *From good things to better*. I have got a lot of fun out of compiling both my volumes in this series and I hope that readers of this new one will find it enjoyable to peruse.

I acknowledge with grateful thanks the loans of groups of postcards from John Procter and from the Royston & District Museum.

1   This aerial view of Royston town centre was taken just after the Second World War. It looks east along Melbourn Street, the line of the ancient Icknield Way. In the centre foreground is the brewery, which was closed in 1948, after which the buildings were used for some years as Barratt's sweet factory. Pollarded lime trees and tombstones can be seen in the churchyard; the trees were later felled and the tombstones moved to line the walls, thereby easing maintenance of the grass.

Birds-Eye View of Royston.

2   Another aerial view, this time looking towards the south up the High Street, on the line of the Roman Ermine Street. Royston Cross is in the centre foreground with Beale's Corner Café and bakery at the south-west corner of the crossing. Towards the top of this picture the large open space is the Warren, where there was still a conglomeration of cottages between the grassed area and London Road. The large house among the trees (top right) was Sun House, later demolished to make way for the residential roads of Hillside and Mounteagle.

3 Taken in the 1930s, this view of the town looks west from the Stile Plantation before the meadow in the foreground became Priory Close. This meadow had been the 'Eldfield' of the Priory in mediaeval times, when it was farmed by the monks. Therfield Heath is on the skyline. Prominent right of centre is the three-storeyed ironmongery of Messrs. Halstead & Kestell in the market place. The large arched and latticed window nearer at hand belonged to the Magistrates' Court in Priory Lane.

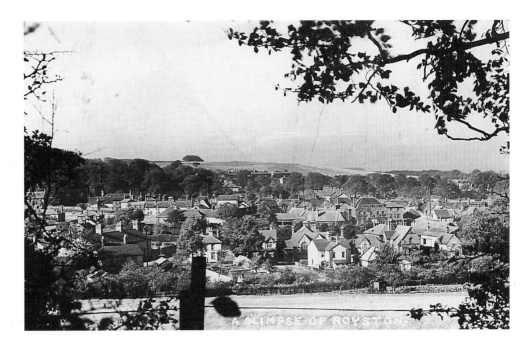

A GLIMPSE OF ROYSTON

4   Stile Plantation runs southward from the Newmarket Road to the Barkway Road and consists principally of beech trees. Originally private woodland, it was presented to the town by Mr. Thurnall and is currently maintained by the Royston Town Council. When this picture was taken, the view to the east was entirely of arable fields stretching away into the distance. Since the Second World War these acres have been replaced by a large residential area comprising the roads that lead off Studlands Rise and Valley Rise.

5   The northwest angle between Stile Plantation and Barkway Road had erected on it in 1908 the orphanage for little girls run by the National Refuges for Homeless and Destitute Children. Between the wars the institution was taken over by the Shaftesbury Society and boys thereafter were cared for there. Many of them went on to the Arethusa training ship to become merchant seamen. This view shows the back of the buildings and their playing fields. After the Second World War the place was taken over by the Inner London Education Authority as a residential school for boys, but it subsequently was closed.

6   The tower of Royston St. John the Baptist Parish Church was cased in flint during the first of the two major church restorations during the reign of Queen Victoria. Previously it had been lath and plaster! The mediaeval church of the priory stretched westwards from the main west door below the tower. The wall seen on the right of this picture is thus a fragment of the south wall of the original nave. The present nave was the chancel of the early building.

Royston Church.

7   The Priory house stands where the monks' Priory formerly stood and the long wall is the remains of the south wall of the nave of the Priory church. After the dissolution of the monasteries in the reign of King Henry VIII the Priory house passed into the ownership of a series of families, most notably the Chesters, who entertained King James I there before he built his Palace in Kneesworth Street. After the Second World War most of the grounds became the Priory Memorial Gardens dedicated to the memory of those who fell in that conflict.

Ye Olde Priory Royston

105474

8   This card clearly shows how narrow were the streets around the old Crown at Royston Cross. Estimates of the width between Beale's Corner Café and the Crown were as little as 12 feet! Kneesworth Street was not much wider at this point. The two cars show how poor the visibility was for drivers and hence how dangerous this important crossroads was, so it was perhaps inevitable that buildings were removed to open up the junction, even though some lovely structures were thereby lost, together with the sense of urban enclosure.

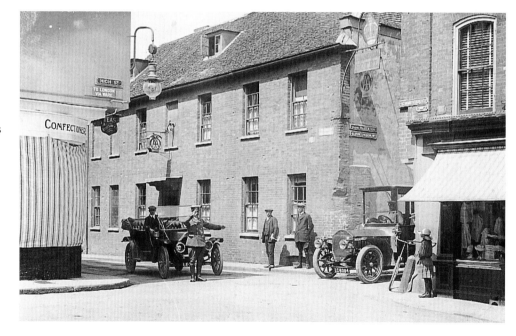

9　When the Crown Hotel at the Cross was demolished for road widening in 1929 an open space was formed and two plane trees were planted. Behind them can be seen the new public conveniences erected at that time and facetiously known as 'Clark's College', after Councillor Robert H. Clark, who was a vigorous advocate of the new amenity.

ROYSTON.

10   The grocery shop owned by the Titchmarsh family stood on the east side of High Street, a little to the north of George Lane. It is seen decorated for, probably, the coronation celebrations of King George V in 1910. When this building and its neighbour, Matthews' pharmacy, were demolished after the Second World War, several very deep wells were discovered beneath them.

11   The High Street changed little during the 1920s and 1930s. Looking downhill the large emporium on the right was Bishop's furniture shop with the offices of Messrs. Nash, Son & Rowley (auctioneers and estate agents) beyond it. These were also the offices of the Royston Water Company.

High Street, Royston.

12   The old cottages at the top of High Street date back to before the reign of King James I, who banned jettied upper storeys as a fire precaution. They form part of the 'middle row' between the two parallel thoroughfares of High Street and King Street. When the market was founded in Royston this was the original site for the stalls. It is common in English market towns for two such narrow streets on either side of a middle row to mark where a market was once held. In the Royston case it is said that it was once possible to go from top to bottom of the High Street through the roofs of the middle row!

OLD ROYSTON

13 The very top of High Street, showing the Chequers and the Bull inns. The chequer may be a reference to the Stuart chequy of black and white, but is probably much older, because the arms of the Priory of Royston carried the same chequy on the sinister side. Again, this is a pre-Jacobean building, judging by its jettied (overhanging) upper storey. The upper storey also has some blank windows – relics of the notorious window tax, when windows were often bricked up to avoid paying the tax on them. Note too the gas lamp on the corner of the Chequers and its offer of accommodation for motorists.

High Street, Royston.

14　Looking east from the Cross along Melbourn Street, Royston Post Office is the large three-storeyed building on the right. Note the advertisement on Henderson's Bazaar for the Herts & Cambs Reporter, otherwise known as the Royston Crow, the local newspaper published in the town since 1855. Clearly the cyclist did not have to worry overmuch about which side of the road to ride on!

Melbourn Street, Royston

15   Royston's first purpose-built post office was used as such until its successor was erected in Baldock Street in 1935-1936. Subsequently it was used as a club for servicemen during the Second World War, then as a community centre, later as a bank, and later still as an estate agent's office. It is said that the town was so quiet at night in Victorian times that a tapping heard in the building one night by the man on duty turned out to be a large spider walking along the post office counter!

16   Outside the old post office in Melbourn Street is a grille in the pavement marking the top of Royston Cave, the entrance to which is across the road. This sketch of the Cave illustrates its bell-shaped form in the chalk. The way down is via a steeply sloping passage dug beneath the street in the 1790s. The original mediaeval access would have been down one of the two shafts near the top of the Cave.

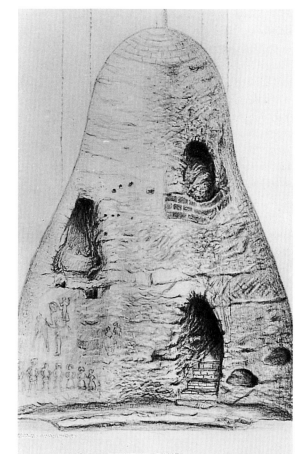

ROYSTON CAVE.

Section of the Cave looking north-east showing the two shafts and present means of access.

17   The Banyers Hotel was originally the home of the Reverend Edward Banyer DD, Vicar of Royston from 1739 to 1752. These were the days when the clergy were second only to the gentry in the hierarchy of society, so that vicarages were substantial edifices. The grounds of the Banyers stretched away to the north as far as Butchers Baulk, the footpath between the Green and Melbourn Road. The meadows forming the part of the estate furthest from the house were eventually developed as the King James Way housing estate.

BANYERS HOTEL, ROYSTON.

H.8191.

18   Banyers and Thurnalls are the most substantial properties on the north side of Melbourn Street. Immediately to the east of them stood the house that was bought in 1916 by an enclosed order of Roman Catholic nuns, the Sisters of Adoration of the Sacred Heart, and became St. Benedict's Priory until 1964. It had a large L-shaped garden with a frontage to Melbourn Road. Most of this area was taken up by the Town Hall/Civic Centre car park and the actual convent site made way for the police station opened by HM Queen Elizabeth the Queen Mother in 1990.

St. Benedict's Priory, Royston.   (front)

St. Benedict's Priory, Royston.   (Back)

19   Looking south from Melbourn Road towards the junction with Melbourn Street/Newmarket Road, one can see a car just leaving Priory Lane, then a narrow lane with the high mediaeval wall of the Priory grounds on its west side. This photograph must have been taken between 1933 and 1938, because the corner of the Priory Cinema can just be seen on the south-east corner of the crossroads. The Cinema opened in November 1933 after its predecessor burnt down earlier that year, and the Priory wall was pulled down in 1938 when Priory Lane was widened to become a main road.

ROYSTON.

20   The Park, a substantial property on the west side of Melbourn Road, stood in large grounds and was acquired between the wars by the Roman Catholic Church for conversion into St. Mary's Park Convent School, where girls were boarded. Day girls were also accepted and day boys up to the age of nine years. The author gained his early education there from the age of 5 years up to 9 years old. Later the premises became a pre-school kindergarten.

St. Mary's Park Convent School.

21 Green Walk is one of the beech woods planted as a plantation some time about 1800. It was presented to the town by Mr. John Thurnall for the enjoyment of the townsfolk to walk in and it runs from Barkway Street to the London Road. Royston Town Council has the perennial problem of managing this woodland, caused by the need to cut out decayed trees in order to make space for replacements.

Green Walk. Royston.

22   Just where the chalk cutting begins on the Newmarket Road runs a parallel track up through a plantation. There is reason to believe that this marks the line of the Romanised Icknield Way. The Icknield Way was originally a prehistoric trackway, but the Romans constructed one of their roads along its line from Baldock to their settlement at Great Chesterford. The route in Royston is Baldock Road – Baldock Street – Melbourn Street – Newmarket Road. East of the town the route diverges from the main road along the lane known as Noon's Folly.

PINE WALK ROYSTON

23   An aerial view of Burloes, whose grounds lie to the
east of Royston. The drive to
Burloes starts at Newmarket
Road just across the road
from the Pine Walk shown in
the previous picture. This
house was built after a fire in
1931 destroyed its predessor,
which had been completed in
1903 by the Bevan family.
Burloes was sold to the New-
man family in 1923 and they
still own it.

Burloes, Royston, Herts.   6190

24   This section of Therfield Heath lies between Stake Piece Road, Wicker Hall and the farm off that lane to Therfield. The field known as Stake Piece was developed for council housing during the 1920s. The only house shown in this photo is what is now the westernmost house on the south side of Sun Hill. Behind it was constructed the housing estate known as Echo Hill. Anybody wishing to understand the origin of this name should call across the valley from the top of Lankester Hill, whence this picture was taken!

Royston Heath.

25 Baldock Street in the 1930s, looking west from the Cross. The new Post Office was built on the site of the garden of the large house which became Hardiman's antiques business. During the Middle Ages this had been the site of the hospital run by the monks and many bones were found during the excavations. The traffic at this time was still controlled by the RAC man, because traffic lights had not yet been installed, in spite of several serious accidents at the crossroads.

26   The curious and excited crowd that assembled in Baldock Street when the brewery (on the right) suffered a disastrous fire on 5th August 1909. Similarly, a large crowd gathered here on the evening of 8th May 1945 to celebrate the end of the Second World War in Europe. On the latter occasion the local fire service let off the last two maroons that they had in stock – saved up from the days pre-war when the volunteer fire brigade was alerted by this means; one bang denoted a fire in town and two bangs meant an out-of-town conflagration.

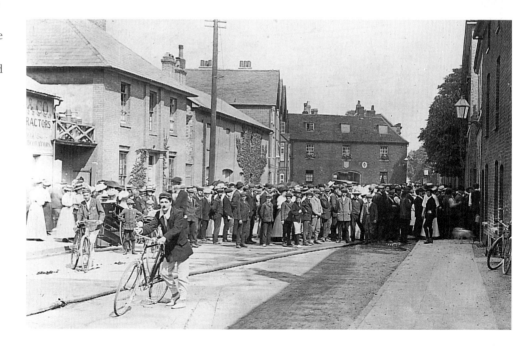

27   This large house on the north side of Baldock Street was The Gables and had been built where an inn known as the Cardinal's Hat had once stood – probably a reference to Cardinal Wolsey, who visited the Priory during the early part of the reign of King Henry VIII. The gates just visible to the right of the house were presented to the town when the house was pulled down in 1961 and were re-erected at the Fish Hill entrance to the Priory Memorial Gardens. Made of wrought iron, they had originally stood at the entrance to the Pickering mansion at Whaddon. The Gables was pulled down and replaced by the Cardinals Hat petrol station, which has latterly been super-seded by a terrace of housing.

28   The Warren is believed to take its name from the area where the monks at the Priory kept rabbits. Introduced into England by the Normans, rabbits were regarded as an acceptable alternative to fish on fast days! Cottages fronting to the Warren on its north and west sides were some of the poorest in the town. Some of their tenants were washerwomen, who hung out laundry on the grassed area. One corner of the Warren was used by a local stonemason to display tombstones; an early example of 'pick your own'!

The Warren, Royston

29   This is the corner of Barkway Street and London Road, where all the buildings were later swept away to improve the A10 main road. On the actual corner stood the Red House, a substantial dwelling. There were cottages next to it in London Road, while in Barkway Street were a row of cottages and two public houses, later replaced by the town's bus station. Further back into the site was a factory used for the making of optical glass in an effort to break the then German monopoly of this material. The costumed characters form part of the 1924 Hospital carnival procession.

30 Division on a point of doctrine led in 1790 to the Nonconformists in Royston forming the New Meeting. Both congregations prospered, so that the Old Meeting outgrew its premises in Kneesworth Street. In 1841 a fire in John Street left a space vacant on which was erected the imposing new home of the Old Meeting. John Street Congregational Church was opened in 1843 and was used until 1922, when the two congregations reunited in the New Meeting's Church in Kneesworth Street. The John Street building became derelict but was used as a store for flour during the Second World War. It was demolished to make way for shops and offices in the early 1960s.

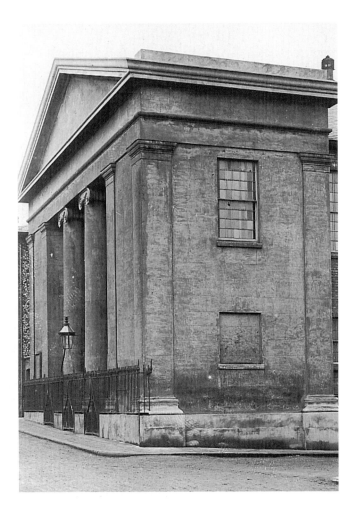

31   Near the Cross in Kneesworth Street stood the Crown
& Dolphin public house. This
odd name is a corruption of
Crown and Dauphin. The site
lies between the palace of
King James I and the lodging
of his son the Prince of
Wales, later King Charles I.
The Prince of Wales being the
eldest son of the King, the
French term Dauphin for the
monarch's eldest son was applied to the name of the hos-
telry, which presumably
existed in the days of the Stuart court. The vertical beam
that supported the inn sign
can still be seen on the front
of the building, now used as
a confectionery shop.

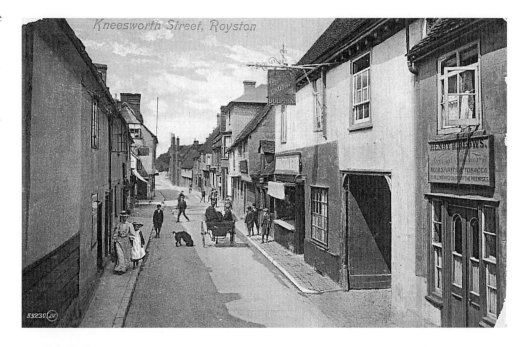

32   Horses were still being brought for shoeing to the forge in Kneesworth Street until around 1950! Mr. Wilson the farrier lived in the jettied cottage next to his business. It is difficult to realise how late the agricultural influence on Royston extended. As recently as the early 1920s flocks of sheep were driven down Kneesworth Street on their way to be loaded on to wagons at the railway station. And, of course, cattle and pigs were sold at the market until well after the Second World War.

33   The elegant garden front of the Old Palace cannot be seen from the street. To build his hunting box King James I had two inns, the Greyhound and the Cock, demolished. The building projected into the street but its western half was pulled down in the 18th century, leaving the two large chimneys which had been in the centre as a prominent feature on the street frontage in Kneesworth Street. Most of the surrounding part of the town was taken over for some purpose by the Court. The Old Palace is a Grade I listed building.

S 8472   KING JAMES PALACE ROYSTON

34   Looking back towards the town centre from near the railway station in Kneesworth Street, it is clear how the 'railway town' was separated from the core of the community. From the Cross to the railway station is nearly half a mile. The building on the right is North Lodge, built in an Italianate style at the end of the Victorian era. Although the street changed little during the early years of the 20th century, one can see that progress has occurred from the large number of wires on the telegraph pole.

Kneesworth Street, Royston.

35   Looking away from the town towards the railway station, North Lodge is now on the left. Beyond it is the Brooklands block of large town houses. The one with the pillared porch was home to Doctor Harold Ackroyd at the outbreak of war in 1914. He volunteered for service with the army, although older than the age at which he might have been expected to serve. He was killed in 1917 shortly after his rescue of a wounded soldier from no-man's-land, an exploit that won him a posthumous Victoria Cross. His name heads the list of dead on Royston War Memorial.

Photo by Robert H. Clark.

KNEESWORTH STREET, ROYSTON.

36   Built in 1912, the Queens Road School was taken over during the Great War for use as a military hospital. The school had been built by the Hertfordshire County Council with an infants' department in the smaller block nearest to the road. The building on the left of the picture is part of the Water Company's pumphouse over their borehole. That on the right is the Mission Hall of the parish church. The site of both school and hall has since been redeveloped as Clark Road (named after Councillor Clark). The blocks of flats there bear the names Mark Hewett House, Vernon Colgan House and Ellen Pyne House. The two former were headmasters of the School and Ellen Pyne left money to build the Mission Hall.

THE SOLDIERS' HOSPITAL, ROYSTON.   *R. H. Clark's Series.*

37 Old North Road is the name applied to the main road northwards from the railway bridge along the line of the Roman Ermine Street. It was once the principal route from London to Edinburgh via York, so it is not surprising that King James I came south this way to take up the throne of England after the death of Queen Elizabeth I. The Great North Road via Baldock later superseded the Old North Road in importance. Houses began to be erected in this part of Royston as part of the 'railway town' in the late 19th century. The Royston by-pass was later constructed across the top of the distant rise.

Old North Road, Royston

38   Looking back up the hill towards the railway bridge, it can be seen that the new housing in north Royston consisted of quite large properties, most of which would have had live-in domestic staff. Side streets also began to be developed as Gower Road and Rock Road. Orchard Road (then known as Garden Road) led off by the hut on the right past orchards to cottages and was not properly made up with a concrete road surface until an aviation spirit depot was established at its western end during the Second World War.

Old North Road, Royston

Robert H. Clark's Series

39   This is Priory Lane in 1938 just after it had been widened to serve as a bypass of the town centre. At first it was one way from north to south; traffic in a northerly direction still travelled down the High Street and along Melbourn Street on its way to Cambridge. The pair of semi-detached houses was built for police families. Behind them can be seen the Priory Close meadow. Note that the mediaeval Priory wall has been replaced by palings!

40   Looking in the opposite direction, the top of Market Hill was also widened and made one-way (towards London) in 1938. The Green Man public house had the main town bus stop outside it, where the double decker can be seen. The house on the corner was occupied by the police sergeant. This was next door to the police station, of which the garage can be seen on the left of the picture. The double-fronted house is 'Abinger', which had earlier been the manse for ministers at the John Street Congregational Chapel.

41　The inn yard of the Bull Hotel shows evidence of several periods. The Bull claims to be the oldest inn in Royston, having almost certainly been in existence in the 15th century. The bow-fronted bay is probably from the 18th century. The ballroom on the left (south) side of the yard is said to have been the assembly room of another inn and was taken down and reassembled to serve the Bull. Between the ballroom and the rest of the hotel was the arch leading through to the High Street and this was the way that coaches came through to change horses for their next stage.

42   The interior of the Bull is typical of old coaching inns, containing dining rooms and bars on the ground floor plus bedchambers on the first floor. After the archway from yard to street was filled in, a new and larger dining room was formed, making use of the space.

The Bull Hotel. Royston.

43   The group of residential roads lying between the railway and Baldock Road is known as the Drifts. This early picture of Green Drift was taken near the junction with Tannery Drift before any development had taken place. It looks westwards along what was then merely a lane leading to meadows and vegetable gardens. Royston Town Football Club at one time used one of these meadows for its ground.

131. Royston, The Green Drift.

44 The Drifts were not made up until some years after the Second World War. They were private roads and their surfaces had deteriorated as the motor vehicle came to dominate transport. The gardens and meadows served by these roads gradually became built up with pleasant houses between the wars. This picture shows Green Drift in the mid-1930s, when development had not proceeded far.

THE DRIFTWAY, ROYSTON.

45   This view is erroneously entitled 'The Grove'. It is in fact Tannery Drift, which runs northward from Baldock Road to intercept Green Drift. There is no sign of the tannery which once was here and gave the lane its name.

Royston — The Grove

46 Lankester Hill on the Heath has often been used as the best place to have a celebration bonfire. This is the one built to mark the wedding of the Duke of York to Princess May of Teck (afterwards King George V and Queen Mary) during the 1890s.

47   The Volunteers were an important part of England's military preparedness over the period from the Napoleonic wars through to 1914. Here are the Royston Company of the Volunteers assembled in the grounds of the Priory around a Maxim (machine) gun. The uniforms indicate that the date was between the end of the Boer War and 1914.

48   The militia encampment held at Whitsun weekend in 1904 took place on the Heath and the volunteers arrived by train at Royston station, from where they marched through the town to the camp site. Here they are coming up the Baldock Street hill and are passing the entrance to Tannery Drift. The large building in the background is the brewery. Note how all the girls are dressed in white pinafores and how nobody has ventured out without a hat!

49   New recruits being drilled at the 1904 militia encampment on the Heath. The military bell tent was the standard accommodation for troops on manoeuvres. There were twenty canvas panels plus an extra flap for the entrance and in theory each man had the space of one panel for his bedroll and kit!

6. MILITIA ENCAMPMENT, ROYSTON, 1904.
"RECRUITS AT DRILL"

PUB BY ROBERT H CLARK.

50   The militia setting out on a route march from the Heath through the town. Preceded by their band, the column is marching six abreast. There are two mounted officers and a cycle messenger. Workers at the brewery have come out to watch.

51   Incidents which would nowadays be recorded in photographs in the local paper were often turned into postcards in Edwardian times. The White Cottage in Tannery Drift suffered a fire in 1905, a circumstance thought worthy of at least three different picture postcards! Perhaps members of the local volunteer fire brigade were the customers for this rather curious publication.

52   This picture shows a car passing through Royston, itself a rare occurrence in 1907. However, in this case the passenger was King Edward VII, a keen motorist, on his way to the racing at Newmarket on 2nd July 1907. The townsfolk turned out to see him go by and he waved cheerfully to them.

53　The first Roman Catholic church in Royston was opened in Serby Avenue on 24th March 1912 in what was little more than a hut. Nevertheless it was opened by the Cardinal Archbishop of Westminster. It served until the new church designed in the Italianate style was completed in Melbourn Road in 1917. This is dedicated to St. Thomas à Becket, whereas the parish church is dedicated to St. John the Baptist.

"His Eminence the Cardinal Archbishop of Westminster at Royston. 24.3.12."

54 Royston Water Company supplied Royston with water from artesian bores at London Road and Queens Road. The latter had been known first as Water Street, because of the pumping station there. This photograph shows men working at the London Road bore on the west side next to Royse Grove. The supply in Royston has always been in-dependent of fluctuations caused by rivers in spate or drought. The Water Company provided the first public sup-ply in the town, which had previously depended upon private wells and rainwater tanks.

55   With the outbreak of the Great War in 1914, casualties were inevitable. This photograph shows the sad return to the town of the first man to be killed in action. The coffin had arrived at the railway station and was escorted up through the streets with full military honours, including the brass band and troops with their arms reversed. Here the procession is just passing Queens Road on its way up Kneesworth Street. The business on the right is McMullen's, who supplied animal feedstuffs.

56   Here the cortege has reached the widest part of Kneesworth Street near the Old Palace. Sadly the town lost 112 men during the First World War hostilities and such ceremonies as this were not repeated. And, of course, many more men were wounded. The loss of over one hundred townspeople from a population of only about 3,500 was not untypical of the nation's experience, but no less traumatic for all that.

57   This 1914 view of
troops encamped on the
Heath shows little difference
from the manoeuvres of ten
years earlier. It looks west-
ward from the edge of the
town to the tents on the lower
slopes of One Hill, close to
the cricket pavilion.

58   Before the days of motor
vehicles used in warfare there
were battalions of cycle
troops. Here such a group has
stopped to rest by West Terrace in Baldock Road, next to
the Tannery Drift junction.
The terrace looked grander
than the accommodation
warranted! Like so many local
buildings, the bricks were
Cambridgeshire whites. Note
the iron railings along the
front of the cottage gardens.
All such railings were removed during the Second
World War for scrap to feed
the blast furnaces. Later West
Terrace was pulled down and
West Court took its place.

59   Front and back of the mascot of Royston Football Club, whose teams have traditionally been encouraged with shouts of 'Up the Crows'. This lad probably held the honour in the days before the First World War. Goalkeeper for the town during this period was photographer Bob Clark (Councillor R.H. Clark), who took many of the originals of the pictures in this book, and who probably took these too.

60   Royston Town Band playing outside the Post Office in Melbourn Street, probably around 1910. The conductor at this time was Charles Hinkins, one of the family who were well known in the town for their music and for their photography. Across the street can be seen a milk float bearing a churn of milk.

61   A group of 'Royston Boys' home on leave for Christmas 1917 got together on Boxing Day in Stamford's Yard off Kneesworth Street. They were, back row: H. Woodcock, Ted Thomas, V. Rowles, Bird, Bird, Jack Gray, F. Sharp, W. Freestone, C. Carter and Carr. Front row: Bird, 'Curly' Humphrey, Stamford, Joe Hamshaw, J.H. Sharp, P. Godfrey and G. Beale.

62   As the Great War progressed, the Royston Crow published a weekly series of short biographies of the local lads in uniform. Many of these were republished as picture postcards, of which this one is an example. It is difficult to comprehend just how large a proportion of the young men of England joined up or were conscripted.

PTE. FRANK WOODCOCK.

Pte. Frank Woodcock, of the Manchester Regiment, second son of the late Mr. J. Woodcock, and Mrs. Woodcock, of 13, Wrexham Terrace, Royston, was reported missing on March 21st. Pte. Woodcock, who is 19 years of age, joined up in February, 1917. He was in training at Dovercourt and Colchester, and was sent out to France on October 29th in the same year. Prior to his joining up he had been employed at the Royston Brewery for about four years. Mrs. Woodcock's other son (Herbert), late of the Oxford and Bucks. Light Infantry, was wounded on August 19th, 1916, and discharged on June 20th, 1917.

Reprinted from . . .   ts. & Cambs. Reporter"
. . .   6th, 1918.

63   Although hostilities ceased with the armistice of 11th November 1918, peace was not celebrated officially until 19th July 1919, when Royston held one of its famous carnival processions, as well as special church services and a variety of entertainments. A large Royston Crow was prominent in the procession.

64   Part of the 1924 Carnival Procession organised to raise funds for the new Royston Hospital, then in course of construction. In the immediate foreground is the 'pack of cards', one of many original and lavishly dressed entries. Crowds came to watch from miles around. Here the procession has reached Melbourn Street and people are standing four deep outside the Post Office.

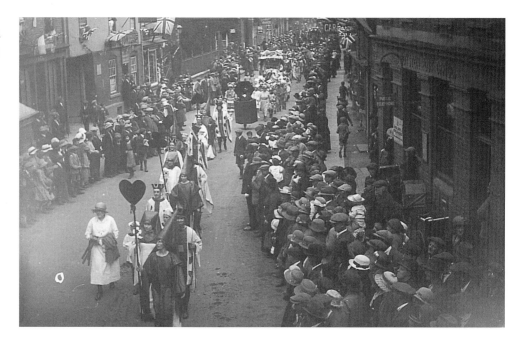

65   May 18th 1928 was a great day for Royston, when the Prince of Wales, later King Edward VIII, came to the town to open the Children's Ward extension to the Hospital. Percival Grundy, who lived at Seven Rides, was the energetic president of the Hospital Committee and is seen here addressing the throng with the aid of that modern contraption the microphone. The Prince is seated on Mr. Grundy's right and can be seen examining his papers. The ceremony was not open to the general public but only to ticket holders!

66 Local businessman 'Dick' Cox was the proprietor of the cinema already, when in 1934 he opened the 'Green Plunge' swimming pool in Newmarket Road near the Town Hall corner and next door to his new Priory Cinema. A café completed the complex, which was well in advance of its time. Cubicles for changing had canvas 'doors'. Male changing was along one side of the pool, female on the other.

Green Plunge Swimming Pool, Royston. Herts.   10544

67 Royston Town Band marching along Melbourn Street in the 1930s, followed by the British Legion, probably on their way to the parish church for a Remembrance Day parade. They are led by Bandmaster Harry Greenhill, wearing his medals. The band is passing Mowberry's grocery shop, which was notable for the frequent smell of newly-roasted coffee beans wafting down the path. The undistinguished building beyond it was the doctors' surgery until the opening of Royston Health Centre in the 1970s.

68 The Royston Branch of the British Legion on parade after winning the Haig Cup in 1934. Again the scene is Melbourn Street. Standard bearer Art Beale is flanked by escorts Bert Foster and Mr. Cosford. Behind them the leader of the marchers is Harry Curtis and wearing caps in the front row are Herbert Woodcock, limping from his war wound, and Arthur Pigg. On the north side of the street are the premises of plumber W.G. Bedwell, the shoe shop of Mr. Pool (who acted as guide to Royston Cave and owned its entrance), and the White Horse public house.

69   James Course (Jimmy), proprietor of the watchmaking, jewellery and optician's business under the clock in High Street, donated a paddling pool to the town's children. It was opened by him on 27th July 1935 and was sited close to the cricket pavilion on the Heath. Sadly it became the target of vandals with broken glass thrown into the water. It was destroyed during the Second World War, when it was incorporated into the prisoner-of-war camp. Walls were built on its coping and the camp's store of coke was kept there!

70   Looking north towards
the Baldock Road, the pool
can be seen to have had an
elegant oval shape and was
initially very popular with
mothers and small children.

The Kiddies Paddling Pool
Royston Heath, Royston, Herts.

145436

71   This is a 1935 picture of the newly-opened paddling pool, looking towards Lankester Hill. The old cricket pavilion, built principally of corrugated iron, is on the left. At various times it was painted red or green. It was eventually replaced by the Sporting Club, which was officially opened in the late 1960s.

72   A band of red indians formed a striking feature in the 1937 procession through Royston to mark the Coronation of King George VI and Queen Elizabeth. They are making their way past the newly-built post office in Baldock Street towards the Heath. The weather was unkind on 12th May, as indeed it was for the corresponding celebrations to mark the Coronation of Queen Elizabeth II on 2nd June 1953.

73   The Priory Memorial Gardens were laid out as a memorial to those from Royston who fell in the Second World War. They were opened in 1949. Here a group of members of Royston Urban District Council have challenged at miniature golf a group of men who raised funds for many projects in the town during and after the war. They are, left to right: R.H. (Bob) Clark, John Banham, F.J. (Fred) Drake, Sergeant Capon, Albert Parrish, Stanley Jackson, Colonel E.C.M. Philips, Mr. Stamford, Ted Shannon, Frank Smith (the author's father), George Langridge, Bill Sheppard, Mr. Spriggs, and Stanley Beale.

74   This card refers to the Royston Crow but actually shows a caricature of the wrong species! The 'Royston Crow', after which the local newspaper is named, is another name for the hooded crow, *corvus cornix*, and has black and grey plumage. Formerly common in the area, it is rarely sighted today in this part of England. The black and white colours adopted by Royston sports clubs derive from the black and grey of the bird. As long ago as the Civil War in the 1640s Roystonians were mocked by troops billeted in the town and were called 'Crows'.

Come to ROYSTON and you will have something to Crow about.

75 Here an unofficial coat of arms has been printed next to an Edwardian view of Royston High Street. This time the plumage of the Royston Crow has been correctly depicted.

76   Royston at last gained an official coat of arms in 1952. The local newspaper, the Royston Crow, led the appeal for funds to obtain the grant of arms, which is here shown at the centre of the card. A Royston Crow standing on the Royse Stone forms the crest. Other references to Royston's history include two Tudor roses, referring to the dissolution of the Priory during the reign of King Henry VIII, the Stuart chequy of King James I, the Hart of Hertfordshire, and the staff of the Prior.